The Marriage Contract

In every business contract everything is clearly written out and signed by each party involved so that there will not be misunderstanding of each person's role and work responsibilities. If there is misunderstanding they can always go back to the contract to clear them up. Not so much in marriage. We sign a contract still and send it into the State in which we live. How often do people actually read that paper? Or really listen and think on the oath and vow they take after the pastor or priest has them repeat.

Together, let's try to solve some of these little foxes that try to steal the love and joy out of marriage.

Song of Solomon 2:15 Good News Translation (GNT)
15 Catch the foxes, the little foxes,
    before they ruin our vineyard in bloom

William and Lillian Johnson in Israel

ACKNOWLEDGMENTS

While Bill was helping me edit my first book, The Final Moments. I had a picture on the front cover of my Daddy James A. Martin who had gone to be with the Lord in 1975, when I was 13 years old. I told Bill when I wrote my next book He would be on the front cover for all the love he had poured into my life. My mother Lillian Martin Johnson Saksek author of God gives Joys to Balance our Sorrows, married Bill in 1976. Bill became My Dad for the next 27 years until he went to be with the Lord 2003. Lillian and Bill were the perfect example of never giving up and working through all the challenges of marriage. I also saw this same resilience and determination to make it through no matter what came their way, (and has influenced my life immensely) is my sister Glenda and her husband Jimmy's marriage of 45 years.

I want to thank my Husband Daniel for the many times he has helped make it possible for me to travel to Maine, whenever family needs or wants me. I am now in Maine for 4 weeks allowing me to write this short handbook.

I want to thank my Brother in-law Henri and Sister Bethany for the many years while I was single allowing me to live with you and help raise your 4 beautiful daughters. Amanda Lillian, Katarina Maria, Victoria Karla, Alexandrea Joelle.

I also want to thank my brother Jimmy Martin and my great nephew Austin Beverage for giving me some insight from a male point of view.

Thank you to my Sister Carolyn for allowing me to use your beautiful picture for my front cover.

Thank you to my Mom, Lillian Saksek, Sister Glenda Beverage and Sister Dr. Mae-Ellen Bailey for last minute editing.

This book was inspired by the countless hours of counseling friends and clients on their realistic and unrealistic expectations of Marriage. So many people have the idea that marriage is going to solve all the loneliness and fill the void in their lives. The biggest problem with this is no one person can fill that void, because it was never meant to be filled by man.   That void can only be filled by having a personal relationship with The Father, Son, and Holy Spirit, by receiving the grace and mercy that comes with acknowledging and asking Jesus Christ into your heart as your personal Lord and Savior.

John 3:3-7 New International Version (NIV)

³ *Jesus replied, "Very truly I tell you, no one can see the kingdom of God unless they are born again.[a]"*

⁴ *"How can someone be born when they are old?" Nicodemus asked. "Surely they cannot enter a second time into their mother's womb to be born!"*

⁵ *Jesus answered, "Very truly I tell you, no one can enter the kingdom of God unless they are born of water and the Spirit.* ⁶ *Flesh gives birth to flesh, but the Spirit[b] gives birth to spirit.* ⁷ *You should not be surprised at my saying, 'You[c] must be born again.'*

Psalm 139:13 New International Version (NIV)
13 For   you   created   my   inmost   being;
you knit me together in my mother's womb.

Romans 8:29
*For those God **foreknew** he also predestined to be conformed to the image of his Son, that he might be the firstborn among many brothers and sisters.*

WOW, God loved us so much He knit us together. How could we not long to know Him? Yet once we enter this world we search so many ways to fill that void. We cannot fill it or expect anyone else to fill it. Only a true personal relationship with God the Father, Son and Holy Spirit can complete us. Now God did say:

Genesis 2:18
*The LORD God said, "It is not good for the **man to be alone**. I will make a helper suitable for him."*

What is a suitable helper?

2 Corinthians 6:14 New International Version (NIV)
14 Do not be yoked together with unbelievers. For what do righteousness and wickedness have in common? Or what fellowship can light have with darkness?

2 Corinthians 6:14 King James Version (KJV)

14 Be ye not unequally yoked together with unbelievers: for what fellowship hath righteousness with unrighteousness? and what communion hath light with darkness?

There are many ways to be unequally yoked not only with unbelievers. Believers can be unequally yoked as well. When we marry someone that has completely different ideas on their role or their spouses role in marriage. This book is designed to help understand your own and each other's expectation of those roles before entering into marriage and hopefully solve some of the frustration that comes when two people become as one.

Example: One gets out of bed first, goes to work. Comes home, walks into bedroom and bed is not made. Gets frustrated; may or may not say anything, yet it opens a door to an argument sometime later.

Other person goes on not having a clue that they did anything to frustrate their spouse. They may have never made their bed, or may felt that was the role of the other spouse. If things like this never get talked about before marriage how are we to know? Communication is up most important.

We all have heard the traditional wedding vow's
I (your name), take thee, (your spouse's name), to be my wedded wife/husband, to have and to hold from this day forward, for better, for worse, for richer, for poorer in sickness and health, to love and to cherish, till death do us part, according to God's holy ordinance; and thereto I pledge thee my faith or pledge myself to you.

WOW. A lot is said in that one sentence. What does it really mean? I am sure each person that reads or says this interprets it differently. Just think about it for a few minutes, what does this mean to you?

Does this mean letting the person just be how they are? Don't we always want to change them a little?
Let's get down to the basics. Making the bed. Whose job is it? In my house it is both our responsibility. If it doesn't get done we don't get upset with the other person. Same with most of the house hold duties.

One of my friends always complained about her husband. He would throw his dirty clothes on the floor in the bedroom. She even tried putting a hamper in the place he threw his cloths. Still he would put them on the floor in front of the hamper. After 5 years of marriage she finally decided to stop nagging about this and within a month's time she realized they seemed to be getting along much better. Some things we are just not going to be able to change about the other person. This is where the better or worse comes in.

Basic things:

Are you going to have a joint checking account?
Are you going to plan to live on 70% of your income?
Put 20% in savings (10 for unexpected things and vacations. 10 for retirement) and 10% for the Lord's house. How does each of you feel about tithing?

Malachi 3:6-12

Breaking Covenant by Withholding Tithes

6 "I the LORD do not change. So you, the descendants of Jacob, are not destroyed. 7 Ever since the time of your ancestors you have turned away from my decrees and have not kept them. Return to me, and I will return to you," says the LORD Almighty. "But you ask, 'How are we to return?' 8 "Will a mere mortal rob God? Yet you rob me. "But you ask, 'How are we robbing you?' "In tithes and offerings. 9 You are under a curse—your whole nation—because you are robbing me. 10 Bring the whole tithe into the storehouse, that there may be food in my house. Test me in this," says the LORD Almighty, "and see if I will not throw open the floodgates of heaven and pour out so much blessing that there will not be room enough to store it. 11 I will prevent pests from devouring your crops, and the vines in your fields will not drop their fruit before it is ripe," says the LORD Almighty. 12 "Then all the nations will call you blessed, for yours will be a delightful land," says the LORD Almighty.

Credit Cards..

Purchases how much can each person spend without consulting each other.

Proverbs 22:7 New International Version (NIV)
7 The rich rule over the poor,
   and the borrower is slave to the lender

Important issues to discuss before marriage who will take responsible for:

Budgeting_____

Book keeping _____

Church _____
Sunday / Wednesday/ Bible study
Time to pray together set aside _____

Date nights _____

Rent or buy_____
Country_____ City_____ State____

Close to Family_____

Holidays/which ones/where_____

Wife work/full time/ part time/ stay home _____

Children/how many/ names _____

How to discipline _____

Home school/ Christian school /Public school

Where_____

Cooking_____

Grocery shopping_____

Dishes_____

Laundry_____

Trash/recycle_____

Will you eat dinner at the table?
What time does each of you think bed time should be?

Are you going to have a TV? _____
If yes, I suggest that one not be in the bedroom. Use your bedroom as a safe haven for peaceful rest. Sharing the highlights of your day, romance, encouragement, and night time prayers.

Dog who is going to clean up his poo. _____
 and all the other duties that come with animals
Cat litter box_____

Horse...Chickens ect.. _____

Garden _____

Indoor Plants _____

I am sure there are many more things we could list here that I haven't thought of.

In The Pursuit of Happiness

So often we seek for our spouse to bring us happiness. There are many times they do. As we watch little things they do, like in this poem my mom wrote early in her marriage to my Daddy who went to be with the Lord when I was 13.

A VALENTINE FOR MY BELOVED
LILLIAN S. MARTIN FEBRUARY 14,1958

DEAR JIM;
THERE ARE SO MAY WORDS, MY DEAR,
BUT NONE OF THEM CAN EXPRESS
HOW MUCH YOUR LOVE DOES MEAN TO ME
AND HOW I WANT YOUR HAPPINESS.
THE MILLION THINGS YOU GIVE TO ME
THAT MEAN SO VERY MUCH.
A GLANCE, A SMILE, A TENDER KISS,
OR JUST THE SLIGHTEST TOUCH.
TO SEE YOU WITH OUR CHILDREN, DEAR,
MY HEART COULD BURST WITH JOY.
I'M PROND THAT I COULD GIVE YOU
OUR GIRLS AND LITTLE BOY.
I SEE YOUR CHILDHOOD IN OUR SON
I WANTED THAT SO BAD!
IT SIMPLY FILLS MY HEART WITH JOY
TO SEE HIM GROW SO LIKE HIS DAD.
LONG DAYS WHEN YOUR ARE GONE TO WORK
TIME NEVER SEEMS TO GO BY
I FEAR IF I SHOULD EVER LOSE YOU,
I'D SHRIVEL UP AND DIE.
YOU OFTEN DO THE SWEETEST THINGS,
(JELLY DOUGHNUTS AND ICE CREAM)
I FEEL SO VERY FORTUNATE FOR THROUGH YOU
GOD HAS FILLED MY EVERY DREAM.

There are so many blessings that come with marriage. Joy and happiness are one of the greatest blessing that come with learning to really enjoy each other in a marriage.

Learning to over look the little things that can irritate and aggravate us can sure make or break a marriage. Trust plays a key role in any marriage.

Deuteronomy 24:5 New International Version (NIV)

5 *If a man has recently married, he must not be sent to war or have any other duty laid on him. For one year he is to be free to stay at home and bring happiness to the wife he has married.*

I know in this day and age it is not practical for a man not to work. Yet this scripture shows the importance of a husband taking time off to spend with his wife. Sundays is a good day for this.

(wives Praise your husband for being amazingly hard workers, not nagging them for working too much, they will only want to be away more.) also budgeting well and not overspending may help your husband feel like he doesn't have to work so much.

Husbands I suggest you read to your wife 5 minutes a day for the first year The book of Mysteries by Jonathan Cahn

Mark 2:27 King James Version (KJV)

27 *And he said unto them, The sabbath was made for man, and not man for the sabbath:*

Ecclesiastes 2:26 New International Version (NIV)

26 *To the person who pleases him, God gives wisdom, knowledge and happiness, but to the sinner he gives the task of gathering and storing up wealth to hand it over to the one who pleases God.*   **Psalm 37:4 King James Version (KJV)**

4 *Delight thyself also in the LORD: and he shall give thee the desires of thine heart*

Matthew 25:23 New International Version (NIV)

23 *"His master replied, 'Well done, good and faithful servant! You have been faithful with a few things; I will put you in charge of many things. Come and share your master's happiness!'*

BUDGETED

Husband net income _____

Wife's net income _____

Expenses we can't avoid:

House payment or rent _____

House or Renters INS _____

House/Land taxes _____

Electric _____

Water /utilities _____

Groceries _____

Cell phone/Internet _____

Car payment _____

Truck payment _____

Car/Truck INS _____

Gas _____

Auto Maintenance/Tags _____

Medical insurance_____

Work Expenses

Childcare_____

Work shoes/clothing _____

Tools_____

Equipment_____

Work INS_____

Work credit card_____

Software subscription_____

Education_____

Student Loans _____

Unexpected expenses _____

Quality of Life/Just for Fun

Toys Boats/Motorcycles/4 wheelers/Snowmobiles/

Bicycles/exercise equipment/ ect._____

Dining out_____

Games_____

Music_____

Fun Money _____

Vacations_____

Special Occasion

Your wedding _____

(be wise this is a very special day yet being in debt for years and paying interest on this can bring a big burden on a new marriage

Party's _____

Gifts_____

Christmas_____

Valentine's day_____

Friends bridal/bachelor party/weddings_____

Important things to think about

Life Insurance _____

Funeral plots/services_____

Wills/Trust_____

God Parents if something happens to both of you.

_____

Acceptable/Unacceptable Behavior

The making or breaking of a good marriage

To love, cherish and respect. Wow that says a lot there! I have found most women need/want to be loved and cherished most of all. Most men need/want to be respected and loved. That said:

Speak respectably to your spouse. Even during arguments. No Name Calling. No I HATE YOU!
DO NOT say the word Divorce. Go into the marriage believing divorce is not an Option. If you think it may be an option you should rethink getting married to this person.

Ephesians 4:26 New International Version (NIV)
26 "In your anger do not sin"[a]: Do not let the sun go down while you are still angry,

Psalm 141:3 New International Version (NIV)

3 Set a guard over my mouth, LORD;
   keep watch over the door of my lips.

Your spouse should be your best friend and the one you share intimacy with this includes conversation, sharing of dreams and desires.

- Talk and text your Spouse often
- Make lots of eye contact when your together
- Make love often this includes kissing each other and saying I love you before leaving the house and when returning home (every time).
- Hug often a slight touch or brush of the hand when walking past each other in the hall or kitchen can go a long way.
- Surprise each other with coffee/breakfast in bed

Exploring Intimacy
Acceptable/Unacceptable Behaviors

Song of Salomon is a great book to read together. I also recommend the Act of Marriage by Tim LaHaye

Song of Solomon 1

The Girl: *[7] "Tell me, O one I love, where are you leading your flock today? Where will you be at noon? For I will come and join you there instead of wandering like a vagabond among the flocks of your companions."*

It is so easy these days to send out a quick text to let your spouse know what you're doing, you would be amazed how romantic this can be.

King Solomon: *[8] "If you don't know, O most beautiful woman in all the world, follow the trail of my flock to the shepherds' tents, and there feed your sheep and their lambs. [9] What a lovely filly you are,[c] my love! [10] How lovely your cheeks are, with your hair[d] falling down upon them! How stately your neck with that long string of jewels.[11] We shall make you gold earrings and silver beads."*

So often you will give each other compliments when you are dating. Within 6 months or so you stop. Unfortunately, you each start to become complacent. I know a couple that have stopped saying I love you. Reason; I married her, she should know it by now. (Say I Love You often)

Hebrews 13:4 New International Version (NIV)

4 Marriage should be honored by all, and the marriage bed kept pure, for God will judge the adulterer and all the sexually immoral.

Hebrews 13:4 King James Version (KJV)

4 Marriage is honourable in all, and the bed undefiled: but whoremongers and adulterers God will judge.

1 Corinthians 7 New International Version (NIV)

Concerning Married Life

7 Now for the matters you wrote about: "It is good for a man not to have sexual relations with a woman." 2 But since sexual immorality is occurring, each man should have sexual relations with his own wife, and each woman with her own husband. 3 The husband should fulfill his marital duty to his wife, and likewise the wife to her husband. 4 The wife does not have authority over her own body but yields it to her husband. In the same way, the husband does not have authority over his own body but yields it to his wife. 5 Do not deprive each other except perhaps by mutual consent and for a time, so that you may devote yourselves to prayer. Then come together again so that Satan will not tempt you because of your lack of self-control.

I have heard those scriptures referred to the marriage bed cannot be defile. That is not true. What this is saying is not to defile it. For example, it is not ok to bring porn or X rated movies into the marriage. I had one client tell me her husband used these two scriptures saying he had the right to chain her up and whip her. This is demonic and is not glorying to God in any way.

1 Corinthians 6:19-20 New International Version (NIV)
19 Do you not know that your bodies are temples of the Holy Spirit, who is in you, whom you have received from God? You are not your own;20 you were bought at a price. Therefore honor God with your bodies.

God created us to have a fulfilling and enjoyable love life.

Intimacy **is one of the greatest gifts God has given us. Honor and cherish it. It is important that both people feel free and safe to enjoy each other.**

Song of Solomon 2:16-17 Living Bible (TLB)

16 "My beloved is mine and I am his. He is feeding among the lilies! 17 Before the dawn comes and the shadows flee away, come to me, my beloved, and be like a gazelle or a young stag on the mountains of spices."

By Glenda Beverage
45 years of marriage
Recipe for a good marriage

Things to Improve your Marriage that Doesn't take time or Money... And you WIN ☺

Eye contact ~ hold it a little longer than you are comfortable with
Kissing~ each time you say hello, good bye, or goodnight
Bragging~ about him to someone else~ BEST when he is in hearing range ☺

Showing Concern for him ~ "you must be beat" "how was your day?" "tell me about your meeting?" What did _____ think about_____? (fill in the blanks) Get him talking by asking questions he can't answers with "yes" or "no".

Sex~ never say no, in fact, surprise him and initiate it ☺ ! (Jump in the shower and wash his back) ☺

Admiring ~ comment to him about the things you admire most in him. "you have such a great sense of humor! You make me laugh when I am feeling blue."
If he's like my husband and answers every question with a question... call him on it. "Why do you answer every question with a question?" It only took about 5 times before he stopped doing it! (after 30 years of not thinking to ask him that question) ☺
God bless you and keep you! I will be praying for you. Love, Your sister in Christ, Glenda

Romans 14 *Living Bible (TLB)*

14 *Give a warm welcome to any brother who wants to join you, even though his faith is weak. Don't criticize him for having different ideas from yours about what is right and wrong.*

In every marriage there is usually one spouse that has a closer relationship with the Lord. We need not to criticize them but to live our lives like Christ to draw them to be more like Christ themselves.

Ephesians 4:29 New International Version

²⁹ Do not let any unwholesome talk come out of your mouths, but only what is helpful for building others up according to their needs, that it may benefit those who listen.

Proverbs 17:17 New International Version

¹⁷ A friend loves at all times,

and a brother is born for a time of adversity.

Seek to become best friends with your spouse.

Romans 12:9-12 New International Version

Love in Action

⁹ Love must be sincere. Hate what is evil; cling to what is good. ¹⁰ Be devoted to one another in love. Honor one another above yourselves. ¹¹ Never be lacking in zeal, but keep your spiritual fervor, serving the Lord. ¹² Be joyful in hope, patient in affliction, faithful in prayer.

Proverbs 6 NIV

Warning Against Adultery

20 *My son, keep your father's command*
and do not forsake your mother's teaching.
21 *Bind them always on your heart;*
fasten them around your neck.
22 *When you walk, they will guide you;*

when you sleep, they will watch over you;
when you awake, they will speak to you.
23 *For this command is a lamp,*
this teaching is a light,
and correction and instruction
are the way to life,
24 *keeping you from your neighbor's wife,*
from the smooth talk of a wayward woman.
25 *Do not lust in your heart after her beauty*
or let her captivate you with her eyes.

NO Texting or spending alone time with the opposite sex.

No matter how innocent it may seem in the beginning you're allowing a door to be opened, when the Lord says don't even go near that door!

Proverbs 5:8-10 New International Version (NIV)

8 *Keep to a path far from her,*
   do not go near the door of her house,
9 *lest you lose your honor to others*
   and your dignity[a] to one who is cruel,
10 *lest strangers feast on your wealth*
   and your toil enrich the house of another.

1 Corinthians 6:18 New International Version (NIV)

18 *Flee from sexual immorality. All other sins a person commits are outside the body, but whoever sins sexually, sins against their own body.*

The Dangers of Drugs and Drinking including prescribed medications.

Ephesians 5:18 New International Version (NIV)

18 *Do not get drunk on wine, which leads to debauchery. Instead, be filled with the Spirit,*

Proverbs 23:21 New International Version (NIV)

21 *for drunkards and gluttons become poor, and drowsiness clothes them in rags*

Mind altering substances can lead to painful words spoken, violence and open a door to demonic influence.

There are many things that can open doors to demonic influence. We even see it in Peter a devoted follower of Christ. So, if Peter could be influenced while he was in the presence of Christ, how much more can we be influenced if we are opening our minds with mind altering substances.

Here in Matthew 16 in one breath Peter declares Christ as Messiah and in the next he is influenced by Satan to block the will of God.

Peter Declares That Jesus Is the Messiah

13 *When Jesus came to the region of Caesarea Philippi, he asked his disciples, "Who do people say the Son of Man is?"*

14 *They replied, "Some say John the Baptist; others say Elijah; and still others, Jeremiah or one of the prophets."*

15 *"But what about you?" he asked. "Who do you say I am?"*

16 *Simon Peter answered, "You are the Messiah, the Son of the living God."*

17 *Jesus replied, "Blessed are you, Simon son of Jonah, for this was not revealed to you by flesh and blood, but by my Father in heaven.* 18 *And I tell you that you are Peter,[b] and on this rock I will build my church, and the gates of Hades[c] will not overcome it.* 19 *I will give you the keys of the kingdom of heaven; whatever you bind on earth will be[d] bound in heaven, and whatever you loose on earth will be[e] loosed in heaven."* 20 *Then he ordered his disciples not to tell anyone that he was the Messiah.*

Jesus Predicts His Death

21 *From that time on Jesus began to explain to his disciples that he must go to Jerusalem and suffer many things at the hands of the elders, the chief priests and the teachers of the law, and that he must be killed and on the third day be raised to life.*

22 *Peter took him aside and began to rebuke him. "Never, Lord!" he said. "This shall never happen to you!"*

23 *Jesus turned and said to Peter, "Get behind me, Satan! You are a stumbling block to me; you do not have in mind the concerns of God, but merely human concerns."*

Knowing this was true of Peter, how much more can it be true of us, when we are filling our minds with the things of the world. Like: Video games, movies, etc. Now I am not saying all games, movies, media and worldly influences are bad. I am saying be mindful of what influences and might distract us. Ask for the gift of discernment.

There are so many things that could still be brought up but in wanting to keep this under 30 pages I am going to close with this:

Ephesians 5 New International Version (NIV)

5 1 Follow God's example, therefore, as dearly loved children 2 and walk in the way of love, just as Christ loved us and gave himself up for us as a fragrant offering and sacrifice to God.

3 But among you there must not be even a hint of sexual immorality, or of any kind of impurity, or of greed, because these are improper for God's holy people. 4 Nor should there be obscenity, foolish talk or coarse joking, which are out of place, but rather thanksgiving. 5 For of this you can be sure: No immoral, impure or greedy person—such a person is an idolater—has any inheritance in the kingdom of Christ and of God. 6 Let no one deceive you with empty words, for because of such things God's wrath comes on those who are disobedient. 7 Therefore do not be partners with them.

8 For you were once darkness, but now you are light in the Lord. Live as children of light 9 (for the fruit of the light consists in all goodness, righteousness and truth) 10 and find out what pleases the Lord. 11 Have nothing to do with the fruitless deeds of darkness, but rather expose them. 12 It is shameful even to mention what the disobedient do in secret. 13 But everything exposed by the light becomes visible—and everything that is illuminated becomes a light. 14 This is why it is said:

"Wake up, sleeper,
rise from the dead,

and Christ will shine on you."

15 Be very careful, then, how you live—not as unwise but as wise, 16 making the most of every opportunity, because the days are evil. 17 Therefore do not be foolish, but understand what the Lord's will is. 18 Do not get drunk on wine, which leads to debauchery. Instead, be filled with the Spirit, 19 speaking to one another with psalms, hymns, and songs from the Spirit. Sing and make music from your heart to the Lord, 20 always giving thanks to God the Father for everything, in the name of our Lord Jesus Christ.

Instructions for Christian Households

21 Submit to one another out of reverence for Christ. 22 Wives, submit yourselves to your own husbands as you do to the Lord. 23 For the husband is the head of the wife as Christ is the head of the church, his body, of which he is the Savior. 24 Now as the church submits to Christ, so also wives should submit to their husbands in everything.

25 Husbands, love your wives, just as Christ loved the church and gave himself up for her 26 to make her holy, cleansing her by the washing with water through the word, 27 and to present her to himself as a radiant church, without stain or wrinkle or any other blemish, but holy and blameless. 28 In this same way, husbands ought to love their wives as their own bodies. He who loves his wife loves himself. 29 After all, no one ever hated their own body, but they feed and care for their body, just as Christ does the church— 30 for we are members of his body. 31 "For this reason a man will leave his father and mother and be united to his wife, and the two will become one flesh." 32 This is a profound mystery—but I am talking about Christ and the church. 33 However, each one of you also must love his wife as he loves himself, and the wife must respect her husband.

Notes, Questions and Ideas

1 Peter (NIV)

1 Peter, an apostle of Jesus Christ,

To God's elect, exiles scattered throughout the provinces of Pontus, Galatia, Cappadocia, Asia and Bithynia, ² who have been chosen according to the foreknowledge of God the Father, through the sanctifying work of the Spirit, to be obedient to Jesus Christ and sprinkled with his blood:

Grace and peace be yours in abundance.

Praise to God for a Living Hope

³ Praise be to the God and Father of our Lord Jesus Christ! In his great mercy he has given us new birth into a living hope through the resurrection of Jesus Christ from the dead, ⁴ and into an inheritance that can never perish, spoil or fade. This inheritance is kept in heaven for you, ⁵ who through faith are shielded by God's power until the coming of the salvation that is ready to be revealed in the last time. ⁶ In all this you greatly rejoice, though now for a little while you may have had to suffer grief in all kinds of trials. ⁷ These have come so that the proven genuineness of your faith—of greater worth than gold, which perishes even though refined by fire—may result in praise, glory and honor when Jesus Christ is revealed. ⁸ Though you have not seen him, you love him; and even though you do not see him now, you believe in him and are filled with an inexpressible and glorious joy, ⁹ for you are receiving the end result of your faith, the salvation of your souls.

¹⁰ Concerning this salvation, the prophets, who spoke of the grace that was to come to you, searched intently and with the greatest care, ¹¹ trying to find out the time and circumstances to which the Spirit of Christ in them was pointing when he predicted the sufferings of the Messiah and the glories that would follow. ¹² It was revealed to them that they were not serving themselves but you, when they spoke of the things that have now been told you by those who have preached the gospel to you by the Holy Spirit sent from heaven. Even angels long to look into these things.

Be Holy

¹³ Therefore, with minds that are alert and fully sober, set your hope on the grace to be brought to you when Jesus Christ is revealed at his coming. ¹⁴ As obedient children, do not conform to the evil desires you had when you lived in ignorance. ¹⁵ But just as he who called you is holy, so be holy in all you do; ¹⁶ for it is written: "Be holy, because I am holy."

¹⁷ Since you call on a Father who judges each person's work impartially, live out your time as foreigners here in reverent fear. ¹⁸ For you know that it was not with perishable things such as silver or gold that you were redeemed from the empty way of life handed down to you from your ancestors, ¹⁹ but with the precious blood of Christ, a lamb without blemish or defect. ²⁰ He was chosen before the creation of the world, but was revealed in these last times for your sake. ²¹ Through him you believe in God, who raised him from the dead and glorified him, and so your faith and hope are in God.

²² Now that you have purified yourselves by obeying the truth so that you have sincere love for each other, love one another deeply, from the heart. ²³ For you have been born again, not of perishable seed, but of imperishable, through the living and enduring word of God. ²⁴ For,

"All people are like grass,
    and all their glory is like the flowers of the field;

the grass withers and the flowers fall,
25   but the word of the Lord endures forever."

And this is the word that was preached to you.

Having Jesus be the head of your house, your heart and your life is the most important decision you will ever make. We see here in 1 Peter how Christ came that we may have Salvation. He is a simple prayer:

God's will is that all will believe in Jesus. Prayer:

Jesus, I do believe that you died on the cross for my sins and the sins of the whole world. Please forgive me for all my sins. Help me forgive anyone that has sinned against me. Will you now come into my heart and become my Lord and Savior? Will you send your Holy Spirit to guide me and open my eyes to your word and your will for my life? Thank you for loving me. Thank you for coming into my heart. Thank you Jesus for all you have done for me. Help me to become more like you. In Jesus' name I pray Amen.

Psalm 19:14 King James Version (KJV)

14 Let the words of my mouth, and the meditation of my heart, be acceptable in thy sight, O LORD, my strength, and my redeemer.

Ephesians 6:12 King James Version (KJV)

12 For we wrestle not against flesh and blood, but against principalities, against powers, against the rulers of the darkness of this world, against spiritual wickedness in high places.

One of my prayers I say often is: I rebuke revoke remove all the schemes of the enemy and I receive decreed and believe all the promises of God.

Another prayer you can say when you are feeling Angry before you allow something to come out of your mouth is:

Anger, Anger, Anger I gather you, everywhere you are in my soul, spirit, and body. I bind you. I repent for my part. I revoke your rights. I cast you to the foot of the cross. Cover you with the blood of Jesus never to return to affect ,e pr anyone else in Jesus Name Amen.

You can say this prayer for any unwanted emotion.

Scriptures to Pray over each other, your family, your home, and your place of employment.

Numbers 6:24-26 (Living Bible)
24-26 'May the Lord bless and protect you; may the Lord's face radiate with joy because of you; may he be gracious to you, show you his favor, and give you his peace.'

Philippians 4:19 (Living Bible)
19 And it is he who will supply all your needs from his riches in glory because of what Christ Jesus has done for us.

Isaiah 41:10 (KJV)
10 Fear thou not; for I am with thee: be not dismayed; for I am thy God: I will strengthen thee; yea, I will help thee; yea, I will uphold thee with the right hand of my righteousness.

Psalm 1:1-3 (KJV)

1 Blessed is the man that walketh not in the counsel of the ungodly, nor standeth in the way of sinners, nor sitteth in the seat of the scornful.

2 But his delight is in the law of the LORD; and in his law doth he meditate day and night.

3 And he shall be like a tree planted by the rivers of water, that bringeth forth his fruit in his season; his leaf also shall not wither; and whatsoever he doeth shall prosper.

Psalm 23:1-3 (KJV)

The LORD is my shepherd; I shall not want.

2 He maketh me to lie down in green pastures: he leadeth me beside the still waters.

3 He restoreth my soul: he leadeth me in the paths of righteousness for his name's sake.

2 Samuel 22:2-3 (Living Bible)

"Jehovah is my rock,
My fortress and my savior.
3 I will hide in God,
Who is my rock and my refuge.
He is my shield
And my salvation,
My refuge and high tower.
Thank you, O my Savior,
For saving me from all my enemies.

1 John 5:18 (Living Bible)
18 No one who has become part of God's family makes a practice of sinning, for Christ, God's Son, holds him securely, and the devil cannot get his hands on him.

2 Corinthians 9:7-8
Amplified Bible (AMP)

7 Let each one give [thoughtfully and with purpose] just as he has decided in his heart, not grudgingly or under compulsion, for God loves a cheerful giver [and delights in the one whose heart is in his gift]. 8 And God is able to make all grace [every favor and earthly blessing] come in abundance to you, so that you may always [under all circumstances, regardless of the need] have complete sufficiency in everything [being completely self-sufficient in Him], and have an abundance for every good work and act of charity.

I have asked the Lord that each and every person that reads this pamphlet will be blessed in their marriage and it will be a beginning guide to a long enjoyable relationship with great communication. May the Lord bless you all with love and health.

Blessed with Love and Prayers
Melody

Made in the USA
Columbia, SC
25 November 2020